The Killer

How To Master It and Achieve

By

Omar Johnson

Copyright 2013 by Omar Johnson. Published by Make Profits Easy LLC

Table Of Contents

Introduction 3

Chapter One: Your Killer Instinct and You 7

Chapter Two: Your Killer Instinct at Home 18

Chapter Three: Your Killer Instinct in Sports 27

Chapter Four: Your Killer Instinct in your Love Life 36

Chapter Five: Your Killer Instinct at Work 48

Chapter Six: Trusting Your Killer Instinct 63

Chapter Seven: Your Entrepreneurial Killer Instinct 77

Chapter Eight: Exercises for Your Killer Instinct 92

Chapter 9: Your Killer Instinct and the Relentless Pursuit of Excellence 104

Chapter 10: Role Models for your Killer Instinct 116

Conclusion 145

Introduction

First of all, thank you for picking up this book. It will change your life. Since you have purchased this book it can be assumed that you know what a killer instinct is and are keen on developing it for the purpose of improving your daily life. It must be stated before proceeding that this book is not about developing actual, literal killer instinct. Strictly defined, that could be fostering sociopathic or even homicidal behavior.

The instinct to kill is inseparable from the instinct to survive and to win. These last two are as laudable as the previous is universally repugnant. Rather than this base instinct, this book is about how to develop the hyperbolic idiom that is common in the world of business and sports; the killer instinct that allows certain individuals to win championships, close sales, and attain position over their peers.

This is something more than aggression or even opportunism, for in the race for success the belligerent and the conniving often fall by the wayside when the people around them discover who they are.

A developed killer instinct is more than a desire to succeed at all costs. Most people desire this, but few are prepared to follow their instincts to win competitions. They listen to reason, and to a society that prizes selflessness and placing the interests of others above their own. There is nothing wrong with this, and the world needs more people that listen to this particular inner voice.

However, if you are reading this book then it is clear that this is not what you want for yourself. You are sick and tired of seeing your more aggressive and assertive peers succeed while you are second best or not even considered at all. You do not want to live the rest of your life sacrificing everything for others only to have disappointment and failure as your reward.

You prize your rational side, yet are puzzled when your rational and reasonable plans fail while the illogical and irrational plots of others seem to bear fruit. There are a thousand clichés that point out the success of the aggressive and the assertive, from this being a dog-eat-dog world to sometimes you will eat the bear and sometimes the bear will eat you. This book is how to eat the bear and be the top dog all in one.

A developed killer instinct is a sophisticated one. Cicero said "The wise are instructed by reason, average minds by experience, the stupid by necessity and the brute by instinct." The aim of this book is not to be the brute, or the stupid, but to be a whole person who recognizes and acknowledges all parts of themselves.

Life experience and a formal education can develop one's rationality, but the killer instinct is something that we all possess, and it is like a muscle that can be exercised. Through the exercises in this book, you will get in touch with this part of yourself and achieve the success that is your birthright. To win at home, at work, at love, or simply to win the battle within yourself. It is all within your reach if you are willing to obey your killer instinct.

Chapter One: Your Killer Instinct and You

So you are probably asking yourself, if a killer instinct is not actually an instinct to kill, what is it and how can it help me? Well, the best way to explain it is that it is the part of you that has the will to win at all costs. More than self-preservation, it is the drive to exceed simple survival and achieve the goals that will make you happy, healthy, and prosperous.

Some people reject this part of themselves, seeing it as cutthroat or anti-social, worried about what others will think of them if they go after what they want. These are the people who struggle throughout life to achieve their dreams, often talking about them but never doing anything to make them happen. Developing this instinct in your everyday life will help you achieve these goals and better you as a whole person.

Know Yourself

In Plato's writings of Socrates, he had his teacher often fall back on a well-established piece of wisdom, and that was "know thyself." Four of the Platonic dialogues use this as a cornerstone of some of the pillars of knowledge in the western tradition.

If you are to function as a whole person, successful and excellent, it is impossible to reject any part of yourself. You have to acknowledge that the killer instinct is within you, and this will require some reflection.

You will most probably have to look back on some parts of your life that you are ashamed of. Some time in your life where you acted selfishly, or you were told that you were wrong for going after what you want. You may have to reflect on your failures. This will not be easy, but you will find that most of the times that you failed it was because you refused to follow your instincts.

You will also find that - at the times when you were - it was only society's weight of guilt and shame that made you push your instincts down. The truth is that society rewards those who go after what they want with wealth and power, prestige and awards. Those that listen to the guilt-voice of society are the ones who are clapping while these few are lauded.

Do Or Die Mindset

You have to realize that the most important thing that you can do in everyday life is act. You will have to do or you will surely die. Those that succeed are those that take initiative. They are the doers, the movers and shakers. They do not possess any special skills or qualities that a million others do not, but they have the will to make it happen for themselves.

They do not look to others to make them successful. They place no belief in supernatural notions like luck or chance. Those that wish for good things to happen for them may occasionally be surprised when it actually happens for them, but those who take it upon themselves to make things happen are the ones who are not surprised by their success. They expect it, they demand it, and when it happens they do not rest on their laurels.

They get up the next morning and make it happen again. You need to develop this mindset, equate failure with death. Use your instincts for self-preservation to your advantage, and use your drive to achieve success to take the actions necessary to succeed.

Break Bad Habits

One of the most powerful forces in the universe is force of habit. Some of these habits that you develop over your life are necessary, and others are simply detrimental. It could be anything from excessive coffee drinking to chewing your fingernails. If a habit is not helping you toward your goal than it is hurting you, and it is not often your rational mind that will tell you when a habit is bad.

You will physically know that smoking is bad for you when you wake up in the morning with a savage cough, but your mind will find a way to rationalize the behavior because you crave the stimulation that the drugs in the tobacco delivers to your brain.

Your instinct is to stop, but your brain tells you to light up again. The same can be said for failure. You want to succeed, need to succeed, and it is your instinct to succeed. Your mind will come up with reasons why you can't. You do not have enough money, you don't have a plan, you aren't from the right family, you don't, you don't, you don't. Your killer instinct is not aware of these so-called obstacles. It is focused on the goal and will cross those bridges when it comes to them.

Know What Behaviors Are Necessary

Another of the most powerful forces in the universe is necessity. You will do what you need to do. Would you eat if it was not necessary for survival? Perhaps you would to achieve pleasure, but would it really be a priority if you could survive without it?

Think of many things that you do in your life and you will be surprised to find how unnecessary many of them really are. Nobody has an instinct that tells them to sit in front of a television for five to ten hours a day. There is little to see in your television that you could not see if you would just get out and live your life.

If you are obsessively watching soap operas, what you really want is to have money and a passionate love affair. Spend that five hours making that happen. It is an instinctual part of you and you will find your way to it if you just go after it.

If a behavior is not conducive to you getting the things that you want, then it is a waste of precious time in your life. You will never get that time back no matter what you do. Just as you know yourself, you must strive to know what necessary behaviors are and which ones are unnecessary.

Save your passion for your interests

Passion. It is like a fire that is inside you, and a powerful force to make things happen. For too many people this passion is wasted. They expend it on things that make them angry or frustrated, on relationships that will never go anywhere, or on a boring career that you hate with a passion. If you have an interest that you are passionate about, you need to focus your passion on that interest.

You may need to break up with a partner who is not supportive of your interests. You may need to quit that job that you are burning up your passion in hating. You need to think of passion as a nonrenewable resource, because when you go home at the end of the day and the tank is empty you will be able to do nothing to further your interests.

Esteem yourself

This may seem self-evident, but those who succeed are usually the ones with self-esteem. It is not the success that brings the self-esteem, but rather the self-esteem that brings the success. You have an instinct in you to esteem yourself and your actions. Your self loathing or obsession with your failures are a learned behavior, from observing others around you or listening to what they say.

Your killer instinct has no capacity to hate anything, least of all yourself. Do not mistake this advice as an excuse to fall into narcissism. Sycophantic self-love is not the same as self-esteem, but is often the mask for the most stunning level of insecurity known to man.

Simply esteem yourself, recognize that you deserve to succeed. You have this capacity within you. It is biologically hardwired, since there is no evolutionary advantage to believe that you do not deserve success or happiness.

Reject The Timid

You may have found in your life that it is easier to just lie down, hang back, let others take the risks and be the center of attention. This may be because of a humiliating public failure or because of a lack of experience that would build confidence.

To be confident and outgoing is more than a matter of not being timid, but rather you have to reject the very concept of timidity. If you reflect on those times in your life when you stayed back and let others go forward to success, you will realize that you were feeling a pull to do it yourself. It was a beast that you had a leash on, and you had to tug that leash pretty hard to keep that beast at bay.

You need to take that leash off. This will not always be easy. You may be a natural introvert and take-charge extroverted behavior will feel incredibly draining. You have to be aware that society is biased against introverted behavior, and that success is disproportionately awarded to the extrovert.

By following your killer instinct, you will find that it will be easier to choose your moment to go against the grain and make an extroverted splash in your introverted pool. Choose the moments when the effort will achieve maximum results that will be worth the expenditure of energy.

You Can't Do Everything, So Do What You Must

All of this together culminates in this central lesson: You have a thousand options to follow every day, and most of them do absolutely nothing to help you achieve success. They are a product of a society that values diversion and entertainment, which is fine in moderation and disastrous in excess.

There is a feeling that we have to do it all, and the simple answer is this: no we don't. While you are sitting on the couch there is a competitor that is burning the midnight oil thinking of ways to leave you in the dust. You may both be following your inclination, but more than likely they are listening to their killer instinct and you are doing everything in your power to drown it out, push it down, and distract yourself from it.

If you take nothing else from this chapter, take this: You can't do it all and anything that you do that does not help you is hurting you. Focus on the path that leads to success. Success and happiness is your birthright, written into your DNA as much a part of you as knowing how to breathe. All you have to do is take a moment, breathe, and let one breath follow the next until your killer instinct begins to develop.

Chapter Two: Your Killer Instinct at Home

Everything begins at home. Your domicile is your castle, your hideout, your base of operations. King Arthur's castle and the Bat Cave all rolled into one. Every component of success in your life is inexorably linked to your home life.

There is a reason why Feng Shui consultants make six figure salaries for rearranging furniture, and it isn't because of mystic mumbo jumbo or ley lines. It is because how you arrange your life at home bleeds into your work life, love life, and every other competition where you are apt to come up short.

You must learn to arrange your home in line with your killer instinct, making it a launch pad to your success by helping you develop the primal drive you have to succeed.

Assess the Situation

The first thing that you should do is step back and take a look at your situation. Walk around your home and take a good look at everything. Observe your furniture, the arrangement of your abode. What do you have in your kitchen? Is your bed made? If you were to meet the most important person in the world, would you be comfortable inviting them into your home? Why or why not?

Even though your home is your castle, it is also a reflection of yourself and it does represent you to others. In order to make changes in your home life to make it in line with your killer instinct, you may need make small adjustments or take drastic steps. You may even need to move out, relocate, and create an environment conducive to success elsewhere.

Be Pragmatic

You will need to be very practical in taking the steps to change your home life. You have to ask yourself these questions. Is it possible? Is it achievable? Do I have the time to do it? Do I have the authority to make it happen? If the answer to any of these questions is no, you have to ask why not? Those "why nots?" are usually the answer to the problem.

You should be able to do any damn thing in your home life that you please. If you are in a relationship with another person who is in direct opposition to the changes you need to make, it may be time to reevaluate your relationship.

If you lack the time to make the changes, you must reflect on what you are spending your time on. Obstacles to the changes that we have to make are barriers to success and will do nothing to help you to develop your killer instinct.

Reduce Clutter in Your Life

By our very nature we collect a great deal of detritus in our lives. Mementos, knick knacks, talismans, and novelties have a way of flooding into our living space until there is literally no more space to live our everyday life.

These are just objects, simple matter made of atoms, and they only have the value that we ascribe to them. However, the more space that they occupy in our lives the less space that is left for us. In order to follow your killer instincts you need room to move and to breathe.

Your space must be your space, not the space of the objects. You may find that you need to eliminate many items from the equation, selling them on Craigslist or taking them to the Goodwill. Once you have reduced this unnecessary clutter you will find that your home now has room for your ambitions.

Simplify Everything Possible

Henry David Thoreau said "Our life is frittered away by detail. Simplify, simplify, simplify!" This is very sound advice because too many times in life we do two or three things at a time to only accomplish one objective that can be accomplished with one action.

A developed killer instinct will seek that straight line that is the closest distance between two points. This is not a case of taking shortcuts, but rather of eliminating unnecessary steps in a process. For example, you may find that it is better when you go shopping not to bother with a shopping list because it takes time to write it down and you are certain of what you want anyway. Time is precious, and anything that gives you more time is more time that you can spend achieving your objectives.

Get Enough Sleep

Part of knowing yourself is being aware of how much sleep you need and making certain that you are giving yourself time for it. If you are not getting enough sleep, your every instinct will be to sleep and it will override your killer instinct.

When a moment comes when you find you need it most, all that you will know is how tired you are and you will miss the opportunity. Someone else will "go in for the kill" while you are focused on how weak your limbs are and how blurry your vision is.

Getting enough sleep is the cornerstone of preparation and one of the most important things that you can do at home to hone your killer instinct. Schedule your sleep time as aggressively as you schedule the rest of your life, and manage your work and play time alike to make certain that they do not cut into the time you use to recharge your batteries.

Cultivate Your Aggression

Aggression may be a part of us all, but it does not seem to come naturally to us all. Although there is a distinct difference between being assertive and being aggressive, cultivating your aggression will make going after what you want so much easier.

You need to create an environment in your home that is conducive to enhancing your aggressive tendencies. Ancient Spartans lived in very austere residences devoid of any comfort in order to harden themselves, and although you do not need to sleep on rock or go without a roof it is imperative that you tailor a lifestyle that will harden you similarly.

Something as simple as a choice to forgo unnecessary decoration or forgo entertainment systems or cushy furniture may go a long way toward getting you in touch with that rough and tumble ruthless warrior inside you that will not hesitate to go for the kill when an enemy exposes a weakness.

Instead of a dining room table, eat on a small table while sitting on the floor as the Japanese Samurai did. Instead of an elliptical for exercise, hang a punching bag. Make every day another day to become more aggressive. Live it as your truth, and it will become true in all parts of your life.

Avoid Distractions

Our homes are filled with distractions. Time wasters and diversions are a huge portion of the economy and new distractions are invented every day. They can range from a gaming system that you play too much to an incontinent pet that you constantly have to clean up after.

It may be hard to let go of these darling things, but you will do what you need to do to be successful, and wasters of your time and energy will do nothing to help this happen. If you have taken all the steps just mentioned, and still find your home backed with diversions and distractions, then it may be time to make further cuts.

Your home is not a pleasure palace. It should be a church to your ambition, with all the austerity and utilitarian design that a church entitles. It should have no altars to anything other than your killer instinct and your will to win. In this house of worship of your coming victory, you need not tolerate any false idols and nonbelievers.

Be Observant

There are words often attributed to Thomas Jefferson stating that "Eternal vigilance is the price of liberty." Although he never uttered these exact words, the meaning is clear. You have to be observant of the things in your life that are contributing to your decline, and these things can very often be found in our everyday home life.

Always be on the lookout for a way that you can improve upon the environment from which you relate to all other parts of your life. In order to go for the kill at work, play, or your love life you must have a home that is a statement of this intent. Winning, as many things, begins at home.

If you see anything that is a distraction, clutter, or otherwise that obstructs you from what you need to do in order to get ready to achieve victory in all you do you cannot hesitate to remove it from your life. It will probably be difficult, but it may be the first and most important time that you use your killer instinct.

Chapter Three: Your Killer Instinct in Sports

When talking about a killer instinct, one of the arenas in life where it is more socially acceptable than in others is in the sports world. It may be pushed down and vilified in other walks of life, but on the field it is celebrated.

No matter what sport you play you will find that a developed and refined killer instinct is virtually the only path to success. You can see it in the eyes of those that have it. It doesn't matter if you are Baltimore Ravens Linebacker Ray Lewis or Golf Legend Tiger Woods. Looking into the eyes of these individuals is a window to focus and ambition that can only come from pure instinct.

You can have this if you work at it. If you have taken the advice of the previous chapters you are probably mostly there. Here, on the field of sports, you have your chance to finally put it into action to the roar of the crowd.

Prepare to be Prepared

You cannot expect your killer instinct to just be there waiting for you as soon as you step onto the field and that you can leave it there when you depart. You have to accept it and develop it at home, in the shower, with every practice. This will be hard work, and at times it will be nearly impossible to be motivated.

You may get out of bed one morning and not be able to work out because of the pain that wracks your body from the exertions of the previous day. You have to push against this with all of your might.

Sun Tzu said "When there is no war, the warlike man attacks himself." This is the essence of preparation distilled into one statement. If you have made yourself physically and mentally prepared by a coordinated attack on yourself your instincts will take over on the field, and the war will come to opponents who have already lost and simply do not know it yet.

Relish Conflict

There is a tendency in the modern world to avoid conflict and resolve conflict. There is widespread relativism and the idea that everybody is right and nobody could be wrong. This is not at all the approach you want to take to sports and competition. It is a zero sum game where you are either a winner with everything or a loser with nothing.

You will only be the winner if you can relish the coming conflict. You need to look forward to it, anticipate it eagerly, and think of nothing but the collision between yourself and another who wants it just as much as you.

Take time every day to visualize it. Do not get ahead of yourself and think of celebration and popping champagne corks, trophies or laurels. Think of the conflict at the moment of the competition, and the pain and struggle that will be involved. Smile to yourself and know that it will be their pain, their struggle, and their defeat.

Attack, Attack, Attack

At the moment of competition, this is when you let it all loose. Somewhere inside you is an animal and you need to let it roar. The animal knows how to win the competition, because winning that competition is all that the animal is for. The animal within either survives and thrives or fails and dies.

Its methods of attacking the enemy can vary depending on the situation, circumstance and the strength or weakness of the enemy. Just remember that every battle is won before it's ever fought, but this shouldn't faze you because you have practiced and prepared. You are now ready to compete and to compete you have to attack.

On the football field, be the hammer instead of the nail. On the baseball field, hit that ball like it is the face of your worst enemy. In golf, look down that fairway like a sniper spotting a target. There is a reason why they call successful performance of a task execution. Your opponent is your prey and it is time to go in for the kill. Attack, and never stop attacking.

Control Your Aggression

There are two kinds of people in the world, those that control their temperament and those that allow their temperament to control them. Getting in touch with your killer instinct does not mean becoming a slave to your anger, rage, or bestial impulses.

You must use your instincts rather than let your instincts use you. Some of the most accomplished killers on the planet, the United States Marine Corps, focus the bulk of their training on self-control. Marines going into battle exhibit "cool" on the battlefield because they have been trained relentlessly to trust their instincts while at the same time maintaining total self-control.

When the field is turned against you, and you have been subjected to failure and pain you will feel the onset of your fight or flight instinct. You will be hit with the adrenaline and the impulses that go with it, but fight or flight is your choice. If you are in tune with your killer instinct you will fight, and you will win, with a controlled output of aggression.

Stimulate Your Mind

The Ancient African warriors like Shaka Zulu and Hannibal believed that a fit body was worthless without a fit mind, and vice versa. You must stimulate learning in your mind to achieve the results that you want on the sports field.

You have to view each new piece of knowledge as an objective that needs to be attacked. You will find that this acquisition of knowledge is another step in the conquest of yourself. It will not dull your instincts, but sharpen them to a razors edge. For your instincts are within your mind, and your mind is like another muscle that needs to be worked out.

Instead of lifting weights, read books. It doesn't matter if your field of study is nothing more than the statistics of the great athletes that came before you or accounts of games that you remember from your childhood. What matters is the end result, a fit mind in a fit body, together becoming a finely tuned weapon driven by instinct.

Minimize Mistakes

Mistakes will be made. This is as certain as the sun rising tomorrow. How you respond to these mistakes is of the utmost importance. You will feel humiliated and humbled by these mistakes. These feelings are of no value. They will get in the way of you going for the kill, make you hesitate at the moment of truth.

You cannot eliminate mistakes, but you can minimize the effect that they have on you by simply moving on to the next play, the next round, the next at bat. That kicker that hangs his head after missing the field goal is giving in to shame, which will lead to despair. There will be plenty of time later to feel either shame or pride. This is a time for neither.

You must look past mistakes and trust that you instinctively know how to make the play. The next time that you have the chance, go for the win without reservations or hesitation.

Don't Give Up

The time will come. The odds will look insurmountable, an enormous point differential that cannot be overcome or a single set before defeat. This is your moment. This is when you realize that the crowd may not care what you do in these last moments but your opponent will remember.

Even in defeat you may get another chance at your opponent down the road, and you must do everything in your power to make sure that they do not look forward to it. Neither victory nor defeat are permanent conditions, and if your opponent will

go home a winner make sure they limp
home with that trophy. Go for the
kill, and make them remember the day
that they faced you.

Enemies-Finish Them!

The time will come. You will look
down on your all-but defeated enemy
and everybody will be suddenly
concerned with sportsmanship. They
will not want you to go for the extra
score because that would accomplish
nothing but humiliating your opponent.
Do not listen to that voice, whether
it is inside you or around you. It is
the pinnacle of respect for your
opponent that you go at them as hard
as you can and recognize that it is
their responsibility to stop you.

You have them at your mercy and
you need to show them that you don't
have it. You need to finish them and
send them packing with the defeat that
they deserve. Put them down and they
will know who you are, and the next
time they face you - regardless of
what they will say to the cameras -
they will not look forward to it.

Chapter Four: Your Killer Instinct in your Love Life

You may be surprised to see this chapter, but I encourage you to stop and think about it for a moment. Is there a single more competitive field than the field of your love life? The competition for mates is a part of our genetic code. There are few things that will have men at each other's throats faster than a dispute over a pretty girl, and nothing ends a friendship between women quite like loving the same man.

Ever since Helen of Troy launched a thousand ships by running away from Menelaus with Paris, Love has been one of the fiercest battlefields in the human experience, and I have not met one single adult that has not earned at least one Purple Heart in this particular campaign. Just like sports, it is a zero sum game.

Anyone who has picked up a flower and played "she loves me, she loves me not" knows that sooner or later you run out of petals. Sooner or later, the game is over and you have either won or lost. There are a million dating books that will give you ridiculous psychological tricks to try on your potential mates. This is not anything you need. You know, deep inside, the way to win over your mate. It is that same killer instinct that helps you get ahead in business and sports, and you just have to listen to it.

Be Confident, not overconfident

Almost everybody knows that a confident person is a more attractive person, but it is a case where there can be too much of a good thing. Disgusting arrogance and ridiculous hubris might be good for a laugh, but it is also good for going to bed alone at the end of the night.

You have to listen to your instincts when it comes to how much self-assurance to display, because to a point it is impressive to your potential mate and after a certain point it can be intimidating or even overwhelming. Dial it back a little if you get that little sinking feeling that things are not going well.

Above all, do not underestimate your opponent. In this case, your opponent is not others who are competing for your potential mate, but the object of your pursuit themselves. They are the only ones who have a say in whether you win or lose this fight. All others are irrelevant.

Make the First Move

If you have to wait for your potential mate to come to you, you have already lost. It is one thing if you are pleasantly surprised by an unexpected proposition, and such a thing is something you should take advantage of. But if you are playing the friend or waiting in the wings for another relationship to be over, you have given up the initiative and will never be the one.

They did not relegate you to being an also-ran. You did that to yourself. If they are in a relationship, disregard it. If they get angry because you do not care about their relationship status, that is good. Anger is passion, and passion trumps pity every time. You have to make the first move because you have to sell yourself aggressively.

Never send the message "We can get together if it is ok with you and you have nothing better to do." The message should be constant and persistent: "You are the one that I want. Other people don't matter, just me and you, anytime and anywhere."

It has to bleed out of you every time you talk to them. It will be in your nonverbal behavior. It will be in your eyes. Look too long and smile too long. Every moment is a moment for you to win or lose.

This is the only game that needs to be played, direct and honest, with no playing on jealousy and no deception. It is a simple, honest, direct expression of interest. Deep down everybody, man or woman, has to admit that this is what they want. This directness is the basis of every fantasy men and women have about each other, and if you consistently take this direct approach you will be that fantasy.

Use Your Aggression

Just like the previous chapter, aggression is your friend and you have to use it. It will help you to be assertive, to project the idea that your wants and desires matter. If you don't believe this, why should anybody else? There is a world of doormats out there to wipe your feet on. Why should you be one of them?

You have to rely on your aggression with great care. Too aggressive an approach, typically called "coming on too strong," can be as unsuccessful as being meek. Your aggressive pursuit of the object of your desire should use this natural instinct as a fuel, not a tactic.

Caveman courtship in this day and age gets you a prison sentence, not the love of your life. Women and men alike enjoy the hint of danger, not the reality of it. If you seem totally harmless, you will be less provocative and less attractive as a mate.

Get in touch with your aggression and admit that your desires are as valid as anyone else's. You should pursue them with all your strength because this does an amazing thing: it makes the object of your affection feel desired, and thus desirable. This is what will make them desire you.

Leave your Comfort Zone

We all have this safe space where we feel comfort, and we do not have to worry about anything other than the occasional pang of loneliness. Ignoring your killer instinct will keep you here, in this lonely pasture, while everyone else is having a blast in the jungle of human lust.

If you have had bad luck in love, or just do not seem to get many opportunities to meet people who interest you, you are spending too much time in this comfort zone. You are probably also comfortable, eating comfort food, and seeking further comfort. It may seem difficult, and it may feel awkward at first. You may have to do something that makes you uncomfortable, like going to a dance club and hitting on random strangers.

It may mean putting the moves on a beautiful single woman or an attractive man in the frozen food section just because the opportunity is there. There are a million opportunities every day to leave our comfort zone and try something to break a romantic slump, but - if you find that all you do is stay at home and check your email for responses from your online dating account - you are missing these opportunities.

If you already know who you want, leaving your comfort zone may be the only way to get them to see you as a potential mate.

Face Rejection

This is where your killer instinct will come in most handy, because this will be the point where you are hurt the most. Rejection is another part of the human experience that is hardwired into our brain to make us feel pain.

Being rejected by a mate gives us that "voted off the island" feeling that leaves us shaken. No amount of ice cream or cake will fill this empty feeling that was just scooped out of you. Only your killer instinct, your desire to win at all costs, will get you there. You may have to redefine your objective, decide that if you cannot be with the one you love you should love the one you are with.

There is no shame in this, and in fact such resilience will make you more attractive to potential mates. You need to look forward to rejection as an opportunity to demonstrate your resilience, and recognize that not all rejection is a permanent failure. A mate that rejects you one night may find you more tempting on another, but if you stay home and don't try how will you know? You have to look rejection right in the face and recognize that your killer instinct is stronger.

Reject Sentiment

There is only one that you want, and no one else seems to matter. That is fine. What you want matters and being honest about what you want is the central truth of why your killer instinct will make you successful.

However, you have to reject the sentimental notion that there is only one person for you. There are no soul mates. The world is creaking underneath the weight of nearly seven billion people. There are nine zeroes in that number. The model of our love life that we seem to follow is as outdated as the rotary telephone.

In a world of so many people, more interconnected than ever before, we are deluged in opportunity. You have to move on from every rejection, and occasionally every success at the point at which it is no longer something that you want. You have to move on to the next thing that you want, and attack the objective just as aggressively as you did before.

The point of relationships is not to sacrifice your happiness to make someone else happy. It is to attain mutual happiness and the state of health that follows. You cannot do this if you cling to outdated sentimental notions of what your love life should be. Your instincts tell you everything that you need to know.

Determine the Outcome

If you are waiting for your potential mate to determine the outcome of your relationship, it is already over. You need to determine the outcome through your own agency. Never let a man or woman that you are interested in keep you on the hook, or treat you as an option while you make them a priority.

If you want to be respected you have to demand respect. If you want love you have to demand love. You make your demands known with every action, every romantic gesture, and every sweet whisper. Everything you do is a message, and it is incumbent upon you to send the right message.

There is no shame in taking your time to soften them up a little, but there will come a moment of truth where you will have the chance to pounce on them like a lion or let them run away into the savannah. When that moment comes, you have to rely on your killer instinct and pounce. Go for the kill, and take down your objective, because in the game of love the meek and the shy get trampled.

Your determination and inability to quit will make you a more attractive potential mate than you can possibly imagine. When the object of your affection says your name to their friends that name will mean strength, and strength is always preferable to weakness. When your mate is finally pinned down and gasps your name, give them every ounce of your passion without inhibition. Let them know with every moment that, in your mind, this outcome was never in doubt.

Always be on Top

Now you are in a relationship. Congratulations are in order. That doesn't mean the game is up and you no longer need your killer instinct. You now have a roost that needs ruling.

Getting into a relationship to be ruled may be tempting, for it may be a kind of comfort to let someone else make all your decisions for you. As was said previously, leave this comfort zone and use the instincts that got you the relationship in the first place.

You need to be navigating and making sure that your relationship is heading in the right direction. If you cannot steer your own relationship in the right direction how do you propose to achieve success in anything else?

The bottom line is, enjoy everything that love can bring you, but never let it make you soft.

Chapter Five: Your Killer Instinct at Work

This is the chapter that most of you have bought the book for, and most of you will skip to this chapter and some will not read another chapter after finishing it. I understand where you're coming from, but this would be a mistake.

The world of work can be a jungle, more competitive than sports and more heartbreaking than your love life. I would wager that better than half of people that are reading this book are doing so because of a disappointment in their career.

Somebody else got the promotion because of your hard work and they didn't take you with them. You were fired because you didn't land that big account. Your manager told you that you aren't thriving because you just are too passive. You are reading this book because you know that you can do better and that you deserve better.

Deep down you know what you are capable of and do not understand why others cannot see it. I believe that too, and this chapter is all about bringing that out in yourself. Keep in mind, however, that without keeping in mind the principles that we have already talked about, or paying attention to those that will be introduced in succeeding chapters, you might find that your career prospects remain bleak.

Work cannot be treated as half your life or as a repugnant necessity, but rather as a logical extension of who you are as a whole person.

Be Ruthless

This is first and foremost. The business world is a hard place that is driven by results, and to achieve those results you must focus on them with a lack of compassion. The modern international corporation doesn't hide its true intention or its main goal. Its only focus is on its bottom line and its only accountability is to its stockholders.

There may be claptrap about corporate culture or public relation campaigns about what is being done to preserve tropical birds, but that is window dressing. Pull back the curtain and you will be horrified by the leering face of naked greed. If you want to succeed you must first have no illusions about who you are working for or why you are working for them. You are not there to make friends. You have enough friends, and if you don't you should buy a dog.

You are not there to find a lover. You are not there to save the world. The world is what it is and will always be so. You are there to earn money and achieve personal fulfillment, and personal fulfillment is not the fulfillment of others.

If you work in the civil service, public sector, or for a smaller business you will still find that the very worst traits of corporations are still evident. The workforce is divided into two kinds of people: the ones who will stab you in the back and the ones that will stab you in the front. You have to beat them at their own game, and the only way that you

will do that is to get in touch with
your ruthlessness.

Empower Yourself

This is the fundamental basis of
everything else that you will do in
your career. If you are waiting around
for someone else to empower you, you
will die a failure. Waiting for
authorization to take charge of
something is the most common career
mistake there is.

You may have this thought in the
back of your mind that if you stick
your neck out to take charge of
something that is not explicitly in
your job description there will be
somebody waiting to cut your head off.
This is a normal anxiety, and it is
also the spokesperson of failure.

One of the first jobs I ever had
was as a lowly file clerk, one step
above an intern. If I just did what
was asked of me I would have made sure
that the coffee pot was full and
everybody had enough printer paper. I
couldn't do that. I took it upon

myself to reorganize the file system to make everybody else's job easier.

At first I got resistance from entrenched clerks that were used to the old system, but in a short period of time I was their boss. If I had listened to their whining and complaining and fallen into line I would never have gotten anywhere at a company that was looking for efficiency and a take-charge individual.

I had a friend who got a job as a receptionist, but made it known that she was a photographer by taking everybody's pictures and making her portfolio conspicuous. After about a year she had a good paying job in marketing and was the staff photographer for the entire company. These are just examples of empowering yourself, and the point of this story is to take the initiative. You know what you are good at. Do not neglect your duties, but rather take every opportunity to go above and beyond without being told.

Embrace Risk

Part of taking initiative and empowering yourself is realizing the element of risk. You may fail in just about anything that you try, because if success was a certainty then everyone would be successful. You have to put yourself in a mindset that risk is a good thing, and that the benefits of overcoming risk and achieving success far outweigh the drawbacks of a little public embarrassment if you fail.

You can recover from a setback, but you will drown in obscurity if you refuse to wade out of it. Alexander the Great conquered the entire known world in his short lifetime by embracing this phrase: "Fortune Favors the Bold." This is a timeless truth because if you refuse to take a risk you are absolutely certain to gain no reward.

A risk, however small the actual chance of success, is a better percentage-play than the certain failure that comes from refusing to act. This is not license to constantly live on the edge and act with reckless abandon, but rather a mandate to listen to your instincts when it comes to assessing risk.

You should do a risk assessment to the extent of your understanding, but at that point you should listen to your instincts. You will instinctively know what you can do and what you are capable of. If every fiber of your being says "no" then you should listen to it, but if that is not the case you owe it to yourself to take the risk if the reward is worth it.

Abandon Emotion

This may be one of the more difficult things for you to do in your career. Your work environment is filled with individuals that will do everything that they can do to push your buttons. They will inspire a gamut of emotions in you: happiness, anger, love and hate. This is not something that they are doing unknowingly. Every person you work with is inspiring the emotion that they are inspiring in you for a particular reason, and such emotions are rarely conducive to success.

If you are best friends with your coworker, it will make it difficult to compete with them for a promotion. If your boss seeks to inspire fear, you will do nothing to earn his respect by obliging him. If you get angry too easily and fly off the handle at your coworkers, nobody will want to work with you.

I have seen many serial job changers bounce from entry level job to entry level job just because they cannot get along with people, and most of the time the root of this is they are allowing themselves to be ruled by emotion. You must proceed through your career with a passion for what you do, but you must abandon emotionalism as the hindrance that it is.

If your coworkers or your boss pisses you off, go home and lift weights, pound on your heavy bag, and plan their career demise with cold, calculating precision. Never tip your hand until the moment that it is too late, and then go for the kill.

See Your Enemy Everywhere

As the saying goes, it is not paranoia if they are really out to get you. Since you can never know the motives of others you should not assume that you can. In psychology, the certainty that you can know another person's motives is called fundamental attribution error.

The sexy girl at the reception desk might be flirting with you because she actually likes you or she may be seeing you as nothing more than a step up on the career ladder. She may even just be bored or seeking attention. Following the impulses that her behavior invites may earn you a sexual harassment complaint. You can never be sure why people do what they do, so you should believe half of what you see and none of what you hear.

Your competitors are going to look out for their interests to the exclusion of all else. Although not all of your coworkers are enemies, not all of your coworkers are competitors. Your instincts will let you know the difference between a coworker and a competitor, and no matter how helpful a competitor appears to be, you must regard their overtures with suspicion.

Machiavelli said to keep your friends close and your enemies closer. The first because useful allies from your coworker pool can help you in a pinch, but the latter is who you really want to keep your eye on. They are the ones who are plotting your downfall, and you should give them no opportunity to do so.

Control the Narrative

The difference between success and failure often depends on who tells the story, and in every case you must control the narrative of your career. It has been said that there is no limit to the good a man can do if he doesn't care who gets the credit.

This book is not about doing Good, but rather about doing well. This is about survival in the shark tank that is the career world. Never,

ever, let a single human being claim any shred of credit for the work that you do. Not your coworkers, not your boss... nobody.

Other than your paycheck, credit is often the only real product of your labor. Make certain that everybody knows the work that you do. If that means that you have to work overtime writing the company newsletter or that you have to toot your own horn in company memos that is just what you have to do.

Stepping aside and humbly pointing out the accomplishments of your co-workers is a waste of breath. If they are serious about their success they will do it themselves. The key to this is not to do it constantly. If you are labeled as a shameless self-promoter it will be a hard label to shake, but even that is preferable to being a drone that gets others promoted.

Your career is in your hands and if you care about it you will do everything possible to make sure that you are the hero of the story.

Choose the Battlefield

Sooner or later your enemies will get sick and tired of you. This is a wonderful moment, because it really means that you have made it. Your killer instinct has taken you this far, but it is at this point when your enemy will set traps. Your instincts will know how to step around them, but this is the point where it becomes more important than ever to not only choose your battles, but choose the battlefield.

If you have a confrontation with a rival imminent, make certain that the confrontation is on turf that is advantageous to you. Analyze their tactics and act accordingly. If the aim of a rival is to publicly discredit you, deprive them of a public display.

If their aim is to prevent their own disgrace, make certain that their flame-out is where everybody can see. In the new full-spectrum workplace, with social networking making a private life even more of a public sphere, stealthily and covertly use every tool at your disposal to make certain that the entire universe knows that your rival bit down hard on the disgusting taste of failure.

When you have denied them the support of others and dragged them into a situation where all of their hard work is hidden underneath their abject failure you have to press your advantage and destroy them. This will not only eliminate a rival, but let your other rivals know what is in store for them.

Capitalize on Successes

You have worked hard to achieve success and made a wide variety of sacrifices to make it happen. You have given up the opportunity for friends and lovers, and perhaps your ambition has earned you implacable enemies. You have stepped on people that perhaps did not deserve it and you have clawed your way through this insane gauntlet on pure instinct. This is not the time to go soft.

If you are now in charge of others, it is because you have worked hard to achieve that position. They will not expect anything from you but strong leadership, and whether or not they admit it strength is what they need from you. If they cannot do their job, there is someone else that can.

Although this may be harsh to an individual it will be better for the team, as high performers resent working with others who do not pull their own weight. There may be others who were once your rivals but now are reporting to you. Reward and promote the most ruthless of these, as they are the best resource that you have.

There will never be a time to rest on your laurels. There will always be another young turk sharpening his knives and waiting for you to falter. Do not be afraid of this, but rather relish the challenge, because in the working world the struggle is never over.

Enjoy your successes, but above all you must capitalize on them. You must turn those successes into money, power, privilege, and position. A typical working adult can sacrifice half of their life to their occupation. Some give up even more of their lives, working overtime and using their free time to advance their career knowledge.

This sacrifice needs to mean something, and you deserve the levels of compensation that reflects the enormity of this sacrifice. Never let anyone tell you what you are worth. You tell them what you are worth, with every word and action, and demand nothing less.

Chapter Six: Trusting Your Killer Instinct

As I said in the previous chapter, those that do not read further are doing themselves a disservice. They will attempt the techniques of the previous chapter and they will fail. They will fail and they will wonder why they could not make their instincts work for them.

The reason is simple: they never took the time to get in touch with their killer instinct and therefore could never learn to trust it. Trusting your killer instinct is not easy because for most of your life one person or another has been telling you not to.

If you want to be victorious in whatever you do you have to learn to trust your killer instinct just as much as you trust the beating of your heart or that you will continue to breathe when you fall asleep. Fail in trusting your killer instinct and you are in turn killing a part of yourself.

Trust your vision

In all aspects of your life you have to trust your vision. You have an idea of what you want out of life. You want a good job with good pay. You want a nice house and a nice car. You want a beautiful woman or a handsome man. You can have all of these things. They are not rare, but rather they are abundant.

They are everywhere and you see them every day. Why don't you have them? It is because every time you see them you ask "Why can't I have that?" and then you answer that question. In trusting your killer instinct you will come to see that your goals, however lofty, are obtainable.

You think that you cannot be a successful Hollywood actor because you are not handsome enough? Tell that to Steve Buscemi or Paul Giamatti. You can't be a NFL Quarterback because you're not 6'5? Tell that to Drew Brees' Super Bowl ring. You can't be a successful author because everything you write sucks? Tell that to Stephanie Meyer or E.L James.

You have to drop the excuses and trust your vision. You know in every cell of your body what you want to be. Your killer instinct will make it happen for you if you only let it. There is no reason why you are not driving to the job you want in the car you want with the mate you want… save the ones that you create for yourself.

Embrace change

Throughout your life things will change. This is an absolute certainty, and there is only one of two things that you can do about it. You can roll with the change or you can let the change roll over you. You have to embrace change, or you will never be able to adapt to it or overcome it.

It is tempting to try to create a safe, stable, boring life. You know that is not what you want, but find yourself settling into it. You have to let that go, shake things up, and let things evolve in the direction that they were meant to.

Is your girlfriend or boyfriend holding you back from the things that you want? Dump them with extreme prejudice. Never dump someone just to get back with them on more advantageous terms. Deep down, they will never forget that you chose something else over them and will use every opportunity to make you feel guilty about it.

Dump them and let them stay dumped, because they are replaceable. Have you been dumped? Revel in your freedom and jump on the next thing breathing. Living well is the best revenge, and a person that dumps you is just as replaceable as a person you dump. Your life, however, is not.

Never live someone else's life, but rather live your own with all of your might. Is your job in the way of your happiness? Float resumes everywhere, and to hell with what everybody else thinks. You are the one that has to live with your life, and everybody else will simply be content to use you until you realize that the only one who is allowed to do that is yourself.

Honor the Power of Your Words

Don't waste your breath. Make every word you breathe have meaning. Too many people have diarrhea of the mouth and let every thought that they have in their head come out of their mouth. You have to realize and honor the power of your words. Your words are strength, and only by listening to your instincts can you determine when to disclose something of importance and when to keep your own counsel. Winston Churchill was right when he said "We are masters of the unsaid words, but slaves of those we let slip out."

The takeaway is that words can give us power and words can take it away. The correctly chosen words can sway large crowds and poorly chosen ones can leave us the object of scorn. It is only when we distrust our instincts that we say these awkward things.

We may be trying too hard to impress someone who is not worth the effort, or we may be succumbing to the nerves that come from our lack of regard for ourselves. Although you have to choose your words carefully, you must also be careful not to unduly censor yourself. Honor the power of your words and trust in yourself, and neither will ever let you down.

Be Tenacious

I have previously stated that you should not give up in the arena of sports, and that is good advice for all sectors of your life. Tenacity is a distinct quality that you have to cultivate in yourself. It is not a matter of continuously trying to progress so much as it is about holding everything together.

It is easy to be shaken when things do not go as planned and things start to fall apart. You have to be determined to be the glue that holds it all together. Everything depends on you, and you have to believe that you can get through whatever adversity is holding you back.

Push through it with all of your might. You will be surprised at how swiftly it stops being a strain and how the rewards begin to pour in. Society is naturally structured to lavish rewards on the tenacious among us. Those that stand their ground and refuse to be moved from a position that they hold are held in a certain high regard regardless of whether they succeed or fail.

Take the last stand of the 300 Spartans at Thermopylae or the Texans at the Alamo or Hannibal's last stand with Rome. Although a situation so dire hopefully will never arise for you, realize that in every situation where you have an opportunity to cut and run there is an equal opportunity to stand and fight. No matter how unpopular your position is, it is your position and there are others that believe in it just as you do.

You will be doing them honor by defending it, and even if you fail they will hold you up in honor and esteem for having tried. If it happens often enough, your assailant will lose the will to challenge you because what they lose in victory will be so much more than what they stand to gain by your defeat.

Have Courage

Fear is a powerful drive, emotion, and instinct all rolled into one. It is inexorably linked to your survival, both literal and societal. Those who ignore it can do so at their peril. What is important to realize is that courage is not the absence of fear. Courage is the ability to face the fear, accept it as a part of you, and deny the impulses that lead you to give in to the instinct.

In many ways, your killer instinct is nature's way of counterbalancing this necessary aspect of your biology. In the early human experience, human beings had to hunt creatures that were fearsome: larger than us or possessing deadly natural weapons or great strength. Our killer instinct permitted us to face these creatures and make them our food.

The instinct to face these unfathomable creatures is still within us the same way that it was with our ancestors. The brave people that you read about everyday do not possess any kind of special quality that you or I do not have.

They do not have less fear, and they do not have more bravery. They were simply able to make a choice. The ability to make that choice is always in your hands, and the more that you face fearsome situations the more that courage builds within you like a muscle that you are building at the gym.

Face Your Fear, Overcome Your Fear, Use Your Fear

This is perhaps just as important as courage. Fear can be a fuel that is as powerful as the killer instinct. Understanding this part of yourself can only enhance your killer instinct.

Fear is an absolute thing that you cannot deny that you possess. You really only have two choices when faced with it: use the fear or let the fear use you. Those who hold to the killer instinct in our nature are not inclined to succumb to fear, because fear never leads to victory.

Do not waste your time on bravado or machismo. That is something that is only useful to give others courage. You have to accept that you are afraid and only then can you sublimate it. Then you will use its raw energy to fuel your courageous actions. These actions can be physical or they can be moral.

They can be as simple as standing up for something that you believe in, or as serious as risking your life. This will cause you a great deal of stress, both physical and emotional, but those that master this ability are the ones that do extraordinary things.

Thomas Carlyle posited that all human beings were incapable of action until they had learned to conquer fear, and that every action no matter how small was a small victory against fear. There is a lot of truth to this, because fear of something that we have never tried before - whether it is kissing a lover or riding a bike - has a level of fear or trepidation involved.

The first time that you ever looked down into a swimming pool, you were probably terrified at the prospect of jumping in. Yet once you learned to swim, that swimming pool became your plaything. This is an analogy that holds to all things you fear, for - just as fear of drowning is allayed by swimming - you can similarly use your fear to keep your head above any situation that you encounter.

Purpose over Consequences

This brings up a very important point, and that is this: what if your fear is justified? This is very possible, as many actions carry with them a variety of dreadful consequences. If you listen to nothing else that I say, though, listen to this: there are always consequences. There are as many consequences for failing to act as there are for acting. Given this, why should you trust your killer instinct? It is because your killer instinct is already aware of this truth.

It knows that if you stick your hand into a fire that you will be burned, or that if you pick a fight with a bigger man you could be hurt. Your instinct also knows what you are capable of. What you have to focus on is this: what is your purpose?

Your purpose should be the first thing in your mind, foremost and central to your decision of whether to act or not. Let your instinct worry about the consequences. In some cases, you will find that the outcome is not as important as it is for you to be true to yourself and act in pursuit of your purpose.

If something is necessary and must be accomplished then it is pitiful to allow fear to stop you from doing it. You will find that if you do not care enough to act in pursuit of your own interests that there is no reason for anybody else to do so.

Do Not Waste Energy on Pity

Speaking of things that are pitiful, you will find that there are few things quite like pity when it comes to wasting your time and energy. Ask yourself this question: do you want to be pitied? I didn't think so, and if you do not want to be pitied why would anyone else want you to pity them? The answer is that they do not.

Those that try to cultivate your pity for them hold the pity in no value. They have another agenda, and are using the pity to further the agenda. There never was a panhandler on the side of the road asking for pity. They wish to have your pity to acquire your money, and it works.

Refusing to pity others can seem cold-hearted, but the reality of the situation is that by refusing to pity them you are showing them the respect that you would demand yourself.

This also goes for yourself in those situations where life is not going your way. When things are going wrong and you feel like you are at the end of your rope. When you start to become tempted to pity yourself... don't bother. It is even more of a waste of time and energy to throw your own pity party.

Refusing to pity yourself builds your respect for yourself, separating yourself from your situation. In the final analysis, pity is either one of two things: something others provoke in us to encourage a desired response or something that holds us back from something that we need to do.

Chapter Seven: Your Entrepreneurial Killer Instinct

Congratulations on making it this far. It may seem like you are only beginning but that is because you have not taken the time to look back at how far you have come. You are about to begin an entrepreneurial venture, and everything that is happening now is a result of the culmination of your efforts up to this point.

You may have found the book useful up to this point in achieving a home life, love life, and working environment conducive to success... but this is a whole new game. The life of an entrepreneur is distinct from what you may have encountered in the business world.

You may feel that you are completely on your own, without a mentor or supportive co workers to keep you going. More than at any time in your life you are going to need to rely on your killer instinct to get you through this time. Whether you are trying to woo venture capitalists, promote a new invention, or writing an innovative business book you will find that those who succeed in entrepreneurism are those who can rely on their instincts.

Be a Solution:

The very first step of moving into any entrepreneurial venture is asking yourself this: what problem am I being a solution for? If you cannot answer this question, than it does not bode well for this venture.

I had two friends who I asked this question, one had a coherent answer (he was going to be a trusted third-party between unfamiliar B2B ventures) another had a flippant remark ("I'm going to solve my financial problems"). I am certain that you can guess which one succeeded and which one failed.

By getting in touch with his own instincts my first friend recognized that it is in human nature to distrust new relationships, and a third party acting as an intermediary provides mutual peace of mind to both parties. He was filling a need.

My other friend had a cool-looking product that looked good on a shelf, and that is where is stayed because he could never find a buyer. In seeking a problem that you would be a solution to, your killer instinct can be a very useful guide.

Diligence is Key:

Your vision is not going to take shape overnight. You are going to have to be patient, and what is more you are going to need to be diligent. You may find that you are constantly having to assess and then reassess the situation as you begin a venture.

New business partners that may join along the way need to be thoroughly vetted. Joint ventures need to be closely examined and appraised solely based on their usefulness and effectiveness.

One of my closest friends watched his business collapse right in front of him because he entered into a poorly planned joint venture that was confusing to his customers and costly in terms of revenue. If you intend to expand your venture to beyond a one-person operation you are going to have to accept that partnerships are necessary.

Where there is no trust there is nothing at all, and no benefit can be realized from a source that is untrustworthy. Hold others to account for what they do, especially if it is in your name or especially on your behalf.

Follow your instincts if they tell you that somebody is not who they say they are or if they are not delivering what they said they would. Your instincts already know if your business partner is a punk or an empty suit, and only your killer instincts will know what to do about it.

Communicate With Your Instincts:

Communication with others is going to be a make or break proposition. If you have others working on your behalf, clearly communicating goals and expectations is going to be the only way that they will be capable of achieving what you want them to. It is your responsibility to provide them with a true purpose, sufficient direction, and realistic motivation. Without these three things being understood by those who are working toward making your vision a reality, everything is lost.

My friend that succeeded in his venture to build an MMA Gym supported by memberships gave his workers all three of these things. He was able to let them know that their purpose there was to make walk-ins into members, he taught them techniques that built relationships with the walk-ins, and he incentivized the process by instituting an innovative profit-sharing model where success in recruiting new members directly impacted compensation.

Walking into that Gym, not one of those trainers acted like a salesman but every single one of them sold. Your instincts will let you know what you have to do to succeed, and your instincts know the best way to communicate with those you need to make that success a reality.

Get in Touch With Your Genius:

I know what you are thinking. It is probably along the line of "I am not a Genius. Those are guys like Einstein and Mozart with towering IQs and they only come once a generation." Well, that is where you are wrong.

The word "Genius" from Latin just means "spirit" and those in that time period believed that not only does every human being possess one but so does everything around us. "Genius Loci" meant the spirit of a place and I am sure that you have all heard stories of "Genies" granting wishes.

While I am not asking you to accept such a superstitious proposition, you must recognize that the people in that time period were more in touch with their instincts than we are in today's world. They also recognized a truth that ordinary people were often capable of contributing extraordinary things to society.

Your instincts will tell you what you are good at, and what this thing is that you are meant to contribute. If Einstein had buckled to necessity and kept working at the patent office instead of answering his inner voice we would not know who he was, and nobody knows what would have become of Mozart had he been content to live the idle life of an aristocrat.

You may not be a Genius, but you have a Genius in you and your instincts will help you get in touch with it to make your wishes come true.

Acknowledge your Heritage:

Never forget where you came from. There are billions of people in this world but there is only one you, and if you are turning your back on your culture or your heritage you are doing it wrong. Your heritage will inform who you are and where you're going with your entrepreneurial venture.

I have a business associate who was able to make a successful business out of merchandising urban fashion because that is who he was. He had grown up on those streets and knew what represented the look as well as what urban youth were looking for in their apparel.

Another person I know just made the best tamales from a recipe her mother gave her and she turned one tamale truck into a franchise. These are just examples, but you must see that your heritage is a strength, and your instincts are trying to tell you this.

You may think that you have to hide parts of yourself or your upbringing to fit in, but if you do this you will be too exhausted to fight the battles you must win in your entrepreneurial venture... because you will be too busy fighting yourself.

Be the Risk Taker:

The good news is that you are already halfway here. As I outlined in a previous chapter, embracing risk is a cornerstone of success, and all entrepreneurial ventures are in themselves a risk.

You have to take it a step further, though, and embody the risk taker. You have to make it a part of who you are, walk it and talk it. Everybody in your new organization needs to know that you are not the one who plays it safe and goes for the sure bet. If that is what you put out there, nobody will feel safe coming to you with a fresh idea or a risky proposition that has a huge upside.

Investors will not give you their money if there seems to be no reward forthcoming, and big rewards are only achievable with equal risk. At the same time, you have a responsibility to your venture, and you have to go with your instincts when they tell you that a potential reward does not warrant the risk.

You are going to meet a lot of people who show you some supremely logical charts that tell you exactly why a proposition is certain to work. Take a glance at those charts and a hard look at the people. Your killer instinct is often the only thing that can come between you and the catastrophe that results from falling for the smoke and mirrors. Remember that even though you are the risk taker you are also the decider, and your decision is final.

Grow a Thick Skin:

You have elevated yourself to a level where you are now a target for criticism, and you have to be prepared for this criticism to come. You may feel that it is not warranted, and sometimes it may seem completely groundless. You have to realize that your competitors have a vested interest in tearing you down.

Expecting them to play nice is naive. Although some will give the advice that you should take the high road in situations like this, it is imperative that you do so by growing a thick skin. You cannot let that criticism bother you or it will eat away at you. This is what they want, so you need to acknowledge the criticism, respond to it in a measured manner if necessary, but personally you must shrug it off.

You have to see it for what it is, and how pathetic it really is. Separate the criticism from the critic, or the only response you will be capable of leveling will be an ad hominem argument. A thick skin is in your killer instinct.

Did you ever meet a lion that cared if you called it a bad lion? No. That is how you have to view yourself, as the leader of a pack that wants the space that you are occupying. As the alpha predator, you have a decision to make: whether to give them battle or deny it to them.

If you are already wounded from their criticism you will find that any battle you have to fight will be that much harder. When your competitors see that their criticism has bounced off of your thick hide, however, they will find themselves unable to press their advantage.

Be Flexible:

The life of an entrepreneur can be tough, and you have to be tougher. The secret to being tough can be summed up in one word: flexibility. Toughness is flexibility, and the ability to bend without breaking.

Inflexibility is fragility, and - no matter how hard you are - you will break under sufficient force. Nearly everyone desires success, but few achieve it and even fewer know how to handle that success.

Find natural ways to deal with your stress, avoiding typical crutches like drugs and alcohol. Be able to take time to blow off steam in a constructive and productive way. Failure to do this can lead to your feeling like a car engine running on maximum with no oil in it. You will break down. No matter how much you love what you do, you need to plan for the day when things may not go according to plan.

Be able to bend the plan without breaking it. If a plan is so fragile that one thing going wrong will destroy the entire plan it is probably not a good plan. Flexibility in planning will be a part of an overall flexibility in your life. You will instinctively know what the pivot points are, as you know that the ulna in your forearm is flexible and your radius is not. Knowing what can bend and what will not is essential to success using your killer instincts.

Sacrifice everything:

Nothing is ever done without a certain level of sacrifice, and to achieve everything you are often asked to sacrifice everything. You will regularly be asked to make hard, painful decisions on a regular basis when you are starting a venture.

At first you will feel like a workhorse, having to do everything yourself and feeling like you have no time for yourself. You have to make these sacrifices, and as you grow and get more people to help you in your quest to launch a successful venture it will only get worse.

You may find that a friend who was there for you in the beginning is not the best person for the job anymore. Your friends and family may want positions where they can ride the coattails of your success. It is often the most difficult thing to say no to those that you love, but if you want to be successful it is necessary that you do so.

This is where your killer instinct will come into play. It may be any number of little things, like killing a low-selling publication that you loved or pulling an item that you were sure would work out if just given a chance. You cannot become more attached to your beloved ideas than to your loved ones. You have to go with what works and is effective.

This will hurt your ego at times and it may leave you feeling disillusioned. You may grow to the point that a successful competitor offers you a buyout that you cannot refuse, regardless of the impact it will have on your workers.

Your killer instinct knows the cuts that have to be made and when they have to be made. Always let others know that it is nothing personal, and that your entrepreneurial life is a separate world from your personal life. When it comes time to make the sacrifices, don't shy away from them.

Chapter Eight: Exercises for Your Killer Instinct

It is one of the most common questions that I get: "What can I do to get in touch with my killer instinct?" What you need to realize is that your killer instinct is not purely a mental process. Although mental factors are extremely important you have to realize that instinct is also a physical process.

Instincts are, after all, inexorably linked to the preservation of your physical well being. Therefore, there are many kinds of physical activity that you can undertake that are highly conducive to enhancing your killer instinct.

Regular exercise can also be of an enormous health benefit and that can be a force multiplier in your quest for success. Being able to worry less about your health will free up a great deal of mental energy for you to devote to other pursuits, and you will find that there is a direct correlation between how physically strong you feel and how strong you feel in your career, your love life, or in any competitive pursuit.

Flexibility Training:

A good place to start, especially if you are just starting out and have lived a sedentary lifestyle, is with flexibility training. Learning and performing basic stretching to elongate muscles and work muscle groups that are very rarely used can prepare you for the physical stresses that are to come.

You will hear many experts tell you that this is just a waste of time, especially if you could be using that time for more intensive exercises, but you have to realize that you only get one body and you can't trade it in for a new one if you break it.

As your body gets more used to flexibility exercises and you find that there is no more stress or pain from performing them you may progress to yoga or other disciplines that can benefit your body by increasing its flexibility. As outlined in the previous chapter, being flexible is inseparable from being tough.

Muscular Strength Endurance:

Once your flexibility is assured and you feel warmed up, building your muscle groups is essential. It is recommended that you start out slowly to learn what your muscles can do. A good way to explore these limitations is through basic calisthenics.

Exercises such as push-ups, crunches, and squats are good places to start, but in each case correct execution of the repetitions is essential to preventing injury. If you are not confident in your ability to correctly perform the repetitions, you may want to look into investing in a personal trainer.

This may seem like an extravagant expense, but as I said before it is always cheaper to invest in preventing injury than in treating it once injury has occurred. A good fitness trainer can also steer you away from discredited and overly injurious exercises such as the full sit up.

While you may feel like doing them because you remember doing them in gym class they can severely injure your lower back.

There are many common exercises like the sit up where the benefit is minimal and the risk is sky high. Avoid these and focus on those with more upside, remembering to push yourself. If you can only do ten push-ups one day, do eleven the next. Constantly do your best to add that additional rep until you find yourself able to perform the exercises easily.

Weight Lifting:

Once you begin to feel the results of your efforts in building your muscular strength endurance, it is time for you to jack up the intensity. You will fail to realize any further results without weight training. Weight training is difficult, painful, and ultimately necessary.

If you are not ready to lift free weights there are many gyms that have a wide variety of weight lifting machines for you to practice with until you feel strong enough to train with free weights. It is recommended that you always lift with a partner whether or not you are using free weights because there is a great benefit to short rests between sets and weight lifting can also be a great social activity.

Your partner can push you to exceed your previous personal bests, and can tell through observation when you are pushing too hard. A good partner can help you both to improve and to reduce your chances of injury. Remember that in lifting weights you are building more than just muscle. You are building your mental toughness, which you will need in many other parts of your life.

Cardiovascular Endurance:

You can begin this at any time during your training program, but be aware that your performance and your results will both be enhanced by an effective weight lifting program. One of the reasons why men typically find it easier to lose weight than women is that they typically have more muscle, and more muscle burns more calories.

It therefore follows that if weight is your biggest hindrance to success in a cardio workout then building muscle is a precondition to cardio success. Your cardio regimen can include any number of methods, but most common involve cardio workout machines. These are a good place to start your cardio regimen because they are adjustable, and you may be able to start at a very low intensity until such a time as you are able to endure a higher level of challenge.

Class-based aerobic workouts including watching fitness videos may have to wait until you have built a stronger cardiovascular system, as such things as spin classes and P90X are not geared toward beginners. They are intense programs geared toward making your body a high performance machine.

Once you have worked on cardio machines for a while you will find that they are becoming too easy and you will feel a plateau in your results. This is when you should make a change and switch to more intense programs.

Swimming:

As with cardio, you can begin a swimming regimen at any time in your fitness plan, but you will realize much better results if you have already worked on your flexibility, muscular strength, and cardio endurance as they all come into play. Swimming is a highly anaerobic form of exercise, and a successful cardio regimen can help you to hold your breath longer without degrading your performance. Swimming works nearly all of your muscle groups and is an outstanding form of exercise, but it can take years of practice to perfect proper swimming form.

If you lack proper coaching, you may never achieve proper form. If you have no background in competitive swimming you may find yourself needing to take classes or register for a masters program in order to have access to the coaching that you will need to have swimming be an effective component to your workout.

Swimming is ideal in that it is a low-impact workout that can be an intensive way to burn a load of calories on days when you may not be able to engage in higher impact exercises due to injury or fatigue. It is also well known for being one of the best exercises for sculpting your body into an attractive shape. Becoming more attractive physically can be a huge help in building your confidence and your success.

Running:

One of the most hated forms of exercise, running is also the most indispensable. Although often lumped in with other cardiovascular endurance exercises, I hold it to be distinct for a couple different reasons.

The first of which is that it is much higher in impact than the typical cardio workout and therefore leads to more injuries, and the second of which is that it stands as its own distinct sport. Running is also as much of a mental test as a physical one. It is a struggle against time and distance, and only your mind can tell you if you've won.

After all, there is an infinite amount of both time and distance. I am not going to tell you that you will never have success with your killer instinct if you are not capable of finishing a marathon, but I will tell you that if the prospect of running a marathon is something you find daunting than it may be a good place to start in testing out your killer instinct.

As with the other exercises, it is best to start small and gradually increase intensity. For the first week, you may decide to only run a mile three days a week, but if you do make certain that it is a mile and a half by the end of the second week. Gradually increasing both the distance that you run and decreasing the time that you are permitted to run the distance is the only way to improve.

Some come very naturally to it, whereas others have to work twice as hard for half the results. It is imperative that every time that you run is an attempt to beat your personal best time. If you cannot compete against yourself you will find that you are unable to compete with anybody else when push comes to shove.

Competitive Sports:

At this point you may have seen a great deal of progress in your training plan, and you will find that you want to put your new body to the test. Your competitive juices are flowing and you desire to test your mettle against other athletes. This is good, because this is your best opportunity to display your killer instinct for all to see.

As stated in the previous chapter about sports, you will find that this is an arena where your aggression will be celebrated. You may be tempted to try very aggressive sports such as Football, Lacrosse, or many others where the wearing of armor is a prerequisite, but keep in mind that this is not necessarily the only way to hone your killer instinct.

You may find that you are able to sharpen your competitive edge just as well playing golf, bowling, or even shooting pool. The important part is to compete and put yourself on the line against another human being in a physical contest.

You may have to try a few different sports to find one that you are good at. Natural talent is something that cannot be taught, and if you find that there is one sport in which you excel you should pursue it with all of your might. It will be the best use of your killer instinct to focus it in the area where it will have the greatest impact.

All of the Above:

While you are free to skip any of the suggested components of a successful training plan just mentioned, be aware that you will be doing yourself a disservice. You will be reducing opportunity and you will be cheating your body. It is understandable to be overwhelmed at first, but as you settle into a training plan it will become second nature and you will find that one success builds on another.

In a way, training is about constantly facing defeat and the limitations of your own body. If you feel defeated at the end of a workout, then you have just had an excellent workout. Constantly smashing against the physical limitations of your own body is what is going to make you mentally tough, and others will find that you are a very difficult individual to compete against once you have achieved this mental clarity and toughness.

You will find that the strength of your resolve will grow with the strength of your body, and your competitors will come to fear you.

Chapter 9: Your Killer Instinct and the Relentless Pursuit of Excellence

What is Excellence?

You may want to achieve excellence, but what is it to you? Figuring that out is the first step toward a relentless pursuit of excellence. Too many times people have a sense that excellence is something that only comes in certain situations, that it can be put away when you don't need it anymore. This is not the case.

You have to be consistent and pursue excellence as a lifestyle, not as a tool to be used in some situations and neglected at other times. Others have the view that you are either excellent or you aren't as if it is an intrinsic virtue instead of a quality that can be learned or developed.

By making the pursuit of excellence the central pursuit of your life you will find that you have become relentless, and you will find that a relentless pursuit of excellence paired with a developed killer instinct is virtually unstoppable.

Being Relentless

You have to be unrelenting in your pursuit of your goals in life, whatever they may be. A relentless pursuit of excellence is characterized by not letting an outcome be final. If you didn't break your personal best in the 50 yard dash on your first try, you have to keep going at it until you do.

Don't leave early because you are feeling that it just isn't your day. You may feel that you are in a constant, pitched battle between your duty and your inclination, and you cannot surrender to what you are inclined to do. If your goals are at all important to you, you must give them everything you have.

You have to prioritize the hard things to do over the easy things. You will often feel that 90% of your effort only achieves 10% of the results, but that hard 10% may be the difference between success and failure, and if the next guy has that 10% in his pocket and you don't then everything that you have worked for will go to him.

Always Believe in Yourself

If you do not believe in what you are doing why should anybody else? Your belief that you deserve the goal that you have set your mind to is instrumental to your success. If you find yourself having doubts, you are not relentlessly pursuing excellence. You have, in essence, just relented.

This wavering will do absolutely nothing for your success, so you need to put it out of your mind. Your killer instinct will let you know exactly what to do. If you need to give a mind-blowing presentation to win the client that you need for your promotion, then you have to believe that not only is it possible but that is achievable.

It is only when you accept this truth that you will be able to really work in a constructive way to make it happen. In this case, belief cannot be an intellectual exercise. It has to be a visceral experience that goes through every cell of your body and comes out in every action that you take. You already know how to believe in yourself, want to believe in yourself, so do it every day and watch the results.

There is Always More To Do

Simply put, there are no days off. If you are working 40 hours a week somebody else is working 60 a week. If you are working five days a week somebody else is working through their weekend. Do they want it more than you? Probably not, but they deserve it more than you. That may seem a little harsh, but you have to devote yourself to your goals and treat them as more than an occupation.

An occupation is something that we do to fill the time, and you have to come at it from the other end. A pursuit is something you use your time to achieve, not something that you achieve when you have time. Your time is your most valuable resource, and you will never get any more of it. You have to invest it in the things that you want the most.

Even if it seems that you have done all that you can there is always more to do. A friend I knew in high school went on to the play in the NFL, and there was never any doubt in my mind that it would happen for him. He practiced and worked out to the point of absolute physical exhaustion, and then his work started.

He would watch film, study the playbook, and when there was nothing else left to do he would mentally visualize the game in his mind. It was what he wanted more than anything else and he achieved it because he was willing to do everything in his power to bring it to pass. This is what you have to do every day, without fail.

Killer Instinct

So where does your killer instinct come in? Well, you will quickly find that you are in a constant battle against your own inclination. Your greatest ally in this battle is your killer instinct, and you are going to need it. When 5pm rolls around and there is still work on your desk, or if you are trying to lose weight and somebody hands you a donut, you are going to need your killer instinct as much as you need oxygen.

It is not enough to want to be successful. Making it happen is going to take a high degree of devotion. Every time you have to choose between what you have to do and what you want to do, you must listen to your instincts and make the choice to do what you have to do. Even if you have to do it in pain, soaked in sweat, tears in your eyes, do the thing that will get you closer to your goal.

How can you say that you really want it or really deserve it if you are not willing to do this. There will come a time when somebody steps between you and your goal. How can you say that you want it if you let them stop you? You have to go at every day of your life like it is sudden death overtime. That level of intensity is only possible with a developed killer instinct.

There is No Downhill

There will come a point where you have striven so hard and so long that you will just want to coast. You will feel the need to put on your slippers and just fall down on the couch. This is a no-coasting zone, my friend. Just because an easy part presents itself doesn't mean that you should dial it back.

Rather, you need to power through it all the faster so that you can get to the hard part. You need to seek out that hard part, because it is the hardest parts that yield the greatest rewards, and the difficulties that build the majority of what you want to accomplish.

There may be a million people in the world that want exactly what you want, but none of them will get it because they are not willing to work as hard on the downhill slide as they are on the uphill battle. Don't be one of them.

You have to make it true in your mind that there is no downhill, no point at which you can let up and take it easy. That period of time will always be what you regret later, when you are inches from your goal and could really use those inches that you gave up earlier just because it was easy.

Keep it up

You may have heard somebody tell you to keep it up in the past. This may have been in a phrase like "keep up the good work." It is important that you repeat this phrase to yourself often. Keeping it up is a way to continue making small, positive changes on a continuous basis. It is an expression of belief and it is actually what your killer instinct wants to do.

Your killer instinct doesn't want to quit, doesn't know how to quit. If you have followed the advice in previous chapters about stripping away diversions and distractions know those things in your life that are keeping you from doing what you have to do.

You will find that it isn't important how inspired you are, because 90% of your success will be perspiration instead of inspiration. If you are not soaked in sweat then there is something wrong. You need to sweat out excellence every day of your life, and be willing to put your shoulder down and push your desires into accomplishment whether you are having a good day or a bad day. You can be sure that you will have plenty of both, but if you are able to realize that both present unique opportunities then the bad days will not seem so very tragic.

Hold it Down

There will come a time when all of this really does become too difficult. You will be tired of this, completely drained. This is the time in your journey where it is all too easy to give up, but you have to hold it down.

Holding it down is the point at which you are in your own personal Alamo. Maybe things have gone hilariously wrong. You may have a sense that you are in a dark forest and do not see a way out. Your rival and enemies are all around you and they are not giving up. They want to make sure that you don't get up after the bell. This is where you have to dig in your heels.

This is that gut-check moment when you will find out if you have the intestinal fortitude to handle anything that comes. If you have been relentlessly pursuing excellence, this is actually the point at which it pays off. This is your time, so much more important than a moment of victory. This is your time to show them that no matter how hard they have worked, it wasn't nearly as hard as you worked. By holding it down it may seem like you are biding your time, but it is also an act of supreme faith that your time will come.

The End is the Beginning

Never surrender to your own satisfaction. You may have achieved what you set out to do, and that award, reward, trophy, or trophy wife may be pretty to look at. I have some bad news for you. You have not arrived and it is not over. You didn't surrender to your rivals or your enemies, or to any other challenges that you faced, so why would you give up your pursuit just because you reached a goal?

You need to move to the next goal, and fast. Your relentless pursuit of excellence must be a lifelong endeavor, a never ending struggle with yourself and others. If you ever reach that point where you feel that things have finally come to an end, it may actually be the end of that part of your life.

You cannot settle into that sense of contentment, however, because all the end represents is the beginning of the next part of your life. Your sports career may be over, so you may want to go into sportscasting. Your academic career may have run its course, so it is time to do something with what you have learned. Only you can decide what the next thing is, but don't wait around waiting for it to show up. Go after the next thing that you want with as much ferocity as you pursued this goal.

Chapter 10: Role Models for your Killer Instinct

At a certain point in your journey you will need somebody to look up to and to emulate. Whether we admit it or not, we all need role models. When trying to develop your killer instinct it is tempting to look up to the very worst people. After all, it has often seemed as if the most successful people have also been the most horrible.

For every altruistic visionary like Nikola Tesla out there inventing alternating current there seems to be a conniving Thomas Edison waiting in the wings to electrocute puppies in order to make people think that the invention is unsafe.

This is not the way that you have to go. There are many positive examples and success stories of those who used their killer instinct for their own success and also contributed to the betterment of the world. Although the greatly abbreviated biographies below cannot do justice to the long lives and the accomplishments of the persons who are highlighted, it is my hope that they may inspire further study of their lives in your quest to better use your killer instinct.

History

Even though world history is filled with Hitlers and Stalins and Maos, there are many role models that, through their striving, channeled their killer instinct to better uses than killing. Here is a small selection of those who did:

Alexander the Great

Alexandros ho Megas III, Basileus Macedon as he was known in Greek, was the first great world leader in the western tradition. He was born to the rule of a small hilly portion of Eastern Europe, but his father had left him with an impressive army and a string of victories against their Greek neighbors.

In his short life he acquired many titles as a result of his victories: Hegemon of the Hellenes(Greeks), Shahanshah of Persia, Pharaoh of Egypt, and Overlord of Asia, but what sets him apart from other conquerors who amassed huge empires, such as Genghis Khan, was that his killer instinct was finely tempered. Alexander destroyed his enemies without needing to descend to barbarism.

Although merciless on the battlefield, he was magnanimous in victory. Many historical luminaries have acquired the honorific "The Great" but none match him. Alexander believed in one world, and was unmoved by any other contrarian view. His view of a single world was very unpopular with his Hellenic troops, who had notions of their racial superiority, but he had to be true to himself.

Although some speculate that this contributed to his death at a young age under mysterious circumstances, they cannot deny that it was also what drove him to conquer the entire known world while most armies were fighting over the rights to grazing fields.

Augustus

When Octavian was born there was no such thing as the Roman Empire or a Roman Emperor, but by the time of his death he would not only be the first Roman Imperator but also be deified and worshipped as a god. He was not a larger than life figure, but rather an ordinary man who just may have been the greatest politician that ever lived.

Known as Gaius Iulius Caesar Octovianus for the greater part of his life as a result of his adoption by Julius Caesar, Octavian had an uphill battle to the pinnacle that he reached. He was known for his ability to make the tough decisions. He had to fight Antony and Cleopatra for the right to his own name since Cleopatra had given birth to Julius Caesar's biological child.

Putting them down at Actium nearly destroyed a Rome that had already suffered civil war and the death of the Republic. Once he was Emperor, he was known for sleeping with the wives of his enemies just for information. He also needed to exile his beloved daughter at one point for her appalling behavior, breaking his own heart.

He once boasted that he came to rule of a Rome that was made of stone and left one that was carved of marble, and this was very true.

He is one of the few rulers in history who truly spent their peace dividend wisely, with a dedication to public works that should shame the politicians of today. Many of the aqueducts he commissioned still function today.

Octavian is known as one of the most relentlessly ruthless and cunning people who ever lived, but he also showed what such a ruthless person could accomplish.

Charlemagne

It is said that Charles I of the Franks was born into the dark ages and left the middle ages to his descendants. Like Alexander and

Augustus before him Charles' successors in no way reflected his greatness. Born to a family who rose to rule mostly due to the reputation of his grandfather - whose victory at the battle of Tours had been enshrined in legend - Charlemagne would more than measure up to the expectations of his rule.

In the most barbaric portion of European history, long after the fall of Rome, Charlemagne not only had to contend with pagan holdouts like the Saxons and the Vikings but also with the maneuvering of his older brother Carloman. He needed to be exceedingly ruthless just to survive this competition, because Carloman was determined to rule alone and was not above making deals with whoever opposed Charles (whether such an alliance was a good idea or not).

It was partially this situation that led Charlemagne to lead 50 battles in his lifetime, one of the highest numbers of any king in history, against a mind boggling assortment of enemies. He earned the name Carolus Magnus from his victories in these campaigns, usually attributed to his enforcement of good order and discipline in his ranks.

Enemies that surrendered to his armies knew that they would not be executed or tortured, and that their property would not be destroyed and their women would not be raped. How Charlemagne conducted his wars was the first beginnings of a code of honor that would be known as Chivalry.

However, this only points to how practical he was in knowing how to win a war. You do not win a war by killing every one of your enemies, only in killing their will to fight. He showed his lack of mercy to his Saxon opponents at the bloody verdict at Verdun, letting his pagan enemies know that they could not expect the mercy he granted to his Christian enemies.

A Christian Europe and a civilized Europe were his twin aims, and he saw them as going hand in hand. Ultimately, it would be his vision that won out.

General George Marshall

No General in the 20th Century was more victorious than George Marshall. In 1945 he literally looked at a world that was ruined at his feet, the highest ranking General in the only nation that had Atomic weapons and the only major power to escape the war without having its infrastructure bombed into oblivion.

The British and the Soviets had both won pyrrhic victories and were bickering over the ruins of Europe. There was no end to Generals who would boast of how much destruction they had caused. MacArthur, Bradley, Patton, and Lemay had all orchestrated bloody campaigns that had turned the world into a graveyard.

All of this had been with the Army that George Marshall built, taking a poorly equipped force of 189,000 and building it into a force exceeding 8 million troops. Marshall was a no-nonsense take-no-prisoners type who once chewed out President

Roosevelt for calling him by his first name.

It would have been very easy for him to be as merciless to his defeated enemies and weakened allies as had been the norm during the war. However, that was not aligned with his vision of the world. Marshall did not believe in the ancient edict of Vae Victis, (woe to the vanquished) but rather saw a world that could be rebuilt stronger and better than ever.

Where others only saw desolation he saw opportunity. This rebuilding is what he threw his efforts into for the rest of his life. A General who knows how to destroy is, after all, a very common thing in history. One who knows how to rebuild from the ruins of war is not only rare, but deeply extraordinary.

As we can see from these examples, a developed killer instinct is tempered with mercy and all the best things in men. A developed killer instinct knows when victory is complete and how to make an ally of a defeated enemy. While an undeveloped killer instinct can destroy kingdoms, it is only the developed killer instinct that can build empires.

Sports

The World of sports is full of profiles of men who would fit the mold of paragons of the killer instinct. It could be reasonably argued that no athlete has much of a chance of being successful without it. The men on this list will have those that love them or those that hate them, but they best represent the killer instinct both in the way that they play the game and the way in which they pursue success in their everyday lives.

Michael Jordan

Who doesn't want to be like Mike? Michael Jordan won big at every level that he played at, and yet still had a habit of keeping track of his missed baskets instead of the ones he made. He had won a national championship in college and an Olympic gold medal before he ever stepped foot on an NBA court, but it was there that he would become a legend.

Always well aware of the thin line between success and failure in the NBA, Jordan is universally recognized as the greatest basketball player of all time. While Magic had Bird and Bryant has James, nobody stood on the same level as Jordan when he was in his prime.

He won 6 NBA Championships, which is more than any of the players aforementioned (Although it doesn't come close to Bill Russell's 11 titles in 13 years that was a completely distinct era of basketball) and his killer instinct was as much in evidence in his actions off the court as what he did on it. He always went after what he wanted, even if that meant leaving basketball to play baseball or to go into management, and came back to play dominant ball just as easily.

No player had ever branded himself as effectively or marketed himself as aggressively as Jordan, and his transition to management (with the

Wizards) and ownership (with Bobcats) shows the business acumen that makes him distinct from every NBA player who has ever lived.

Although the younger players of today might one day dream to be the majority owner of an NBA franchise, it is only because Michael Jordan blazed that trail for them.

Tiger Woods

Love him or hate him, in the world of Golf Tiger Woods stands alone. In fact, in terms of dominance of his sport he may stand alone in the world of sports. No athlete has been recognized as the best player in his sport for as long consecutively or in total as Woods.

His streak of number one rankings is such that he could probably never play again or never win again and yet might never be surpassed. How did he recognize this level of success? By applying his killer instinct to himself and attacking himself as viciously as he would any enemy.

Greatness is the point at which talent meets focus, and Tiger Woods sharpened that point until it was razor sharp. He was an instant success coming into the pros, but that was only the end result of a lifetime of focus on nothing but golf. He was better at age 12 than many professionals at the height of their career.

This unquenchable desire to be the best has been applied to every facet of his life, from the way that he brands himself as a model of determination to the ruthless way that he negotiated some of the most lucrative endorsements in the history of sports. Even with the troubles that his career suffered in recent years, with the dissolution of his marriage brought on by his relentless pursuit of women, Tiger Woods will probably never be surpassed either as a sportsman or in financial terms.

If he had one failing in life it was that he was never satisfied in his performance with women, and even in that pursuit his drive and determination is admirable.

Michael Phelps

The Olympics have given us so many extraordinary athletes in so many sports how do you choose just one to talk about? In the realm of accomplishment and domination of his sport, Michael Phelps stands alone. With more medals than any Olympian in history (18 gold medals alone) and 39 world records he achieved a level of domination that put a lot of doubt in minds of people that he was actually doing it clean.

However, he passed all nine of the tests administered to him in the 2008 Olympics, a level of scrutiny that exceeds most professional sports. Phelps drive and determination is obvious, but when it comes to his personality he is very austere and Spartan in his outlook.

His competitive focus gave others very little to talk about other than to comment on how solitary a person he is. His practices were often closed as he did not tolerate distractions and the intensity of his training did not leave room for socializing.

Phelps realized that in order to achieve his full potential he would have to sacrifice everything and be a bit rigid to others. When one of his childhood idols, Ian Thorpe, made a comment to the media doubting his ability he could have wilted under the criticism but instead he stuck the comments on his locker for motivation.

8 Gold Medals later Thorpe had to eat his words. This was only one of three consecutive Olympic games that he dominated, and even in retirement he earns more money in endorsements than the top ranked swimmers currently in contention.

Tom Brady

Tom Brady's success in the NFL was not a sure thing. Playing the most competitive and cutthroat position in sports, he was also burdened by the weight of being a sixth round pick who had needed to fight just to get off the bench his first two seasons at Michigan.

Conventional wisdom had him firmly placed as a career backup or journeyman Quarterback, but he would be universally recognized as the best draft pick of all time. With a career Quarterback Rating of 96.6 as of 2012 he was among the most efficient Quarterbacks in history, and although he led his team to as many Super Bowls as John Elway he won more of them.

Since he took over the starting job for the New England Patriots they have owned their division, taking home 10 division titles. Throughout his career Brady has also been a subject of scorn and envy for his lifestyle, which has included dating supermodels and Hollywood actresses.

There has always been a sense that he doesn't deserve what he got, just being a pretty boy who got lucky when Drew Bledsoe suffered a life-threatening injury. Brady took the opportunity that was given him for everything it was worth, and everything that he has accomplished ever since, from an undefeated regular season to three Super Bowl rings, has been a product of his commitment to excellence and need to win at all costs.

Quarterbacks don't go from being a 6th rounder to being a two time MVP and 8 time Pro Bowler without having a spine made of steel.

All of the men just mentioned have faced adversity and came out the other side as champions. The sports world is full of stories like theirs, of focused competitors and amazing athletes. When you choose a role model for your killer instinct you might not need to look much further than the roster of your favorite local team, for every new season is an opportunity for a new champion to emerge.

Business

It could be argued that the business world is more competitive than either war or sports. The stakes are enormously high and the penalty for failure is immense. Success in the business world does not always go to the smartest guy in the room or the one with the best idea. The saga of Thomas Edison and Nikola Tesla goes a long way to prove this. Who is the last man standing in the boardroom is often determined by who is the most ruthless.

There are no shortages of success stories or examples of cutthroat competition in business, but here are some short profiles of men that you certainly would not want to compete against:

Sam Walton

Some businessmen start businesses and other businessmen form empires that change an entire industry. That is the legacy of Sam Walton. Walmart completely changed the game of how retail stores functioned and its success story is a testament to both the vision and the ruthless edge of its founder.

He grew Walmart from a mom and pop grocery store into a juggernaut of a company that is the largest private employer in the largest economy in the world. He followed a model of a big fish eating smaller fish until that big fish was finally a whale.

Even when he was worth billions he fostered an image that he was an everyday guy who drove a pickup truck, just a working man like every worker in his store. His model of success early in life was to be aggressive, to talk to people before they had a chance to talk. In a society that prizes having the last word Sam Walton knew how important it was to have the first word.

He controlled the conversation the same way that he controlled his image, by being proactive and setting the tone. Although he had a mantra of ten simple rules for building a business, all of these rules were simple common sense. He realized that automating processes and hiring less skilled labor for less money was the key to lowering costs and raising profits, and he pursued it aggressively.

It took a ruthless man to lower prices and wages to the point that no other store could hope to compete with Walmart, and Sam Walton was just the man to do it. Walmart may have been the enemy of the worker and organized labor, but Walton successfully positioned it and branded it as a friend of hardworking families who needed necessities at lower prices.

This logic busting strategy is the essence of who Sam Walton was, shaking your hand with a firm grip and letting you know what he wanted you to know before you even had the chance to think of a question to ask.

Bill Gates

This year Bill Gates reclaimed the title of the richest person in the world, and given that he is in semi-retirement and running charitable endeavors this is a testament to the financial behemoth that the founder of Microsoft created.

His climb from software developer to entrepreneur and eventually CEO is one of the great American success stories. He worked hard enough in school to get into Harvard, and had enough faith in himself to drop out and start his own business even though his business was in a field that was virtually nonexistent.

While everyone else was focused on manufacturing hardware he realized that the true fortune was to be made in making those machines work with software. He rode the wave of the personal computing revolution by positioning himself as a gatekeeper between the manufacturer and the user, where the real money was to be made.

Gates worked tirelessly, sometimes personally reviewing every line of code that the company sent out, and he expected the same of every Microsoft employee. His management style was as confrontational as his business model, and he would challenge every one of his employees to defend their position.

His vision of Microsoft was to expand into every market that it could achieve a foothold in, and destroy their competitors even if they had to do it by giving away for free what the competitor had to charge for. This led to the demise of companies such as Netscape, who despite fielding a superior product could not compete with one that was a free part of an operating system.

Gates business strategies were fueled by his killer instinct which was bent on crushing his competitors, putting them out of business and extracting humongous profits from the marketplace. After numerous complaints by his competitors and foes that Gates ran a monopoly, the United States government intervened with an Anti-trust lawsuit against Gates and his Microsoft Empire.

Even in the face of this Gates did not relent, but rather met it head on with the same determination with which he had built the company. Bill Gates is arguably the most successful person who ever lived, and he did not get there by backing down from a fight.

Jeff Bezos

In 1994 Jeff Bezos turned his back on a successful career on Wall Street to drive cross country to Seattle. On the way, he wrote a business plan that would forever change the way that people shopped. He chose Seattle because the state of Washington had very few potential consumers, a proposition that would have been laughable in the previous century.

Bezos knew two things that made this a strength instead of a weakness. The first being that the Supreme Court had just passed a ruling that online retailers did not need to collect sales taxes except from a state in which they had a presence, and the second was that by selling nationwide he would be able to charge sales tax only to the relatively small population of Washington.

This was one of many well-considered business moves that would build Amazon.com into the largest retailer in the world. Bezos had figured out an important thing that his competitors had not, and that was that in the old model a customer needed to get in their car and drive to find a lower price. By 1994 this could be accomplished with a click of a mouse. More than ever before in history, the customer was king.

Instead of being afraid of this prospect, Bezos was determined to exploit it. He envisioned a bookstore where it was possible to visit and order any book title in existence because the amount of titles that could be carried was not limited to space in a warehouse or a store, but could virtually be any title in existence.

Within 10 years the word title could be replaced with the word item, as Amazon took that model and sold virtually everything. His competitors grumble that he just got lucky, but while they were building warehouses he was shipping from his garage. Bezos instinctively understood that the strength of eCommerce was its freedom from the conventions and limitations of the retail industry.

You could literally sell what you didn't have so long as you were fast enough to ship it to your customer on time. Once this was perfected it was all a matter of keeping the customer happy, and nobody does this better than Amazon. The Dot-com bubble of the 1990s burst, leaving the corpses of Amazon's competitors strewn all over the nation, but Bezos was standing on top of that pile because his instinct was to give the customer not only what they wanted, but what they didn't even yet know that they wanted.

Mark Zuckerberg

Of all the men on this list, all of who followed their instincts and knew how to give people what they wanted, they might all be trumped by Mark Zuckerberg. A student of the classics, psychology, and computer science he figured out a way to sell us back to ourselves and capitalize on our own narcissism.

He is only one of five official founders of Facebook (and other claimants who were forced to settle) but he is the face of a company that smashed its competition by its simple understanding that the website was not the product. The product was the customers, and the social network that they provided was just the framework that their customers would fill in.

Zuckerberg understood that people wanted to be known, if not famous, and that all that he needed to do was create the showcase and the show would provide itself. Sometimes he needed to cut ties with dearly treasured friends when he judged that they were no longer an asset to the company, such as the case of Eduardo Saverin and Sean Parker, and he did not shy away from these tough choices.

His competitors in those early days: Myspace, Friendster, and Hot or Not have all been smashed into irrelevance because they were gimmicky and lacked the insight of Zuckerberg's company. As a student of Harvard, Zuckerberg discovered that the value of the education that he was receiving was in direct proportion to how exclusive it was perceived to be.

While Myspace championed inclusiveness and meeting a deluge of new people, Facebook built itself on exclusion. A member of Facebook had total control over who they wanted to belong to their particular clique, turning the entire world into an enormous high school. This understanding of the darker aspects of what humanity really wants is what makes Zuckerberg a paragon of the killer instinct.

All of these men collectively have this in common: they trusted their instincts and they followed them to a level of success that boggles the mind. Whether in war, sports, or business they knew how to go in for the kill and when to do it because of this trust.

They did not lack compassion, and in every case these men were charitable and great humanitarians in their own right. They were able to be great humanitarians because they were successful, and they were successful because they did not let others get in their way.

Alexander could not have united a world in the face of Persian despotism, so he smashed it under the feet of the world's best infantry. Augustus could not unite the Mediterranean world in a Rome ruled by squabbling oligarchs, so he brought them to heel at swordpoint.

Charlemagne could not unite Europe under a common culture and religion while tribalism was the ruling body, so he tamed it from the saddle of a warhorse. General Marshall could not have rebuilt Europe or Asia while the Axis powers were dancing on the graveyards they created, so he bombed them into oblivion.

In sports and business the role models profiled in this chapter utilized this tactic with every problem and obstacle that they faced. They were successful because they did not let their competitors define what they could or could not do. They were willing to make personal sacrifices to see their vision through, and that is why they reaped the rewards that they did, from Alexander's piles of Persian gold to the IPO of Facebook.

Conclusion:

"Trust your instinct to the end, though you can render no reason."

-Ralph Waldo Emerson

So we come to the end. I said at the beginning of this book that it would change your life, and I am confident that it will. If you are able to follow the examples in this book you will go after what you want, achieve what you want, and be able to finally be proud of yourself and your accomplishments.

It may not be in the areas that the book focused on. Perhaps, with reflection, you find that you really want to better the lives of others and find that a developed killer instinct can make you a tireless defender of the rights of the homeless.

Perhaps you will turn your killer instinct to attacking social ills or those that would use race or sex as a reason to hold others down. There is nothing that says that the application of these principles is selfish in and of itself.

It is all a matter of truly knowing what you want and what your must do to achieve it. If these are ultimately unselfish aims, than you have my admiration. There are only a few parting pieces of advice that I have for you:

Be Patient

The transformation that you seek will not happen in a day. It will be something that you have to work on. There are many factors that contribute to the suppression of you killer instinct. You may find the processes outlined for developing it to be uncomfortable, or even painful.

This is like when you first start working out and feel every muscle in pain, but this pain will be inside you. You have to view this pain as personal growth, as pain leaving your body. In time, with patience, it will become easier.

Recognize Patterns

You need to look at the way your life has gone up to this point, and see patterns that emerge. Do your romantic or career choices always fizzle out the same way? There is probably a reason for it. Breaking patterns and doing the unfamiliar may be the only way for you to utilize your instinct to its fullest, and it is impossible to break a pattern if you are unaware of it. Take a hard look at your decisions up to this point and resolve to act differently in your future opportunities.

Own your Decisions

You will meet too many people who make a decision and then blame others when things go to hell. If you are to trust your decisions you are also to take responsibility for their results. If a decision that you make in the workplace ends in a fiasco, both your boss and your coworkers will respect you more if you own your part in it.

If you fall short in a sports game, don't shift blame for the results that you contributed to it. Did a romantic relationship fail? There were two people in that relationship, and you have to take stock of the decisions you made that contributed to that. You will find that if you do this it will be easy to regain your footing and move on to the next opportunity, whether you succeed or fail.

Be your Role Model

This book gave several role models for you to emulate, but if you are to succeed it will be counterproductive to strictly compare yourself to them. You have to look at yourself with the same respect and reverence that you give to them. Don't be the idol worshiper... be the idol.

You will find in time that you will be a role model of excellence to others and that your success will be written about in a book like this.

Thank you for reading my book... now what are you waiting for? Go out there and get 'em.

The End

Other Books Available By Author Available On Kindle, Audio and Paperback

How To Create A Profitable Ezine From Scratch

The Secrets Of Making $10,000 on Ebay in 30 Days

The Complete Guide To Investing in Gold And Silver: Surviving The Great Economic Depression

How To Sell Any Product Online:"Secrets of The Killer Sales Letter"

How To Make A Fortune Using The Public Domain

Search Engine Domination: The Ultimate Secrets To Increasing Your Website's Visibility And Making A Ton Of Cash

Creative Real Estate Investing Strategies And Tips

How to Make Money Online:"The Savvy Entrepreneur's Guide To Financial Freedom"

How to Overcome Your Self-Limiting Beliefs & Achieve Anything You Want

The Secrets of Finding The Perfect Ghostwriter For Your Book

The Creative Real Estate Marketing Equation: Motivated Sellers + Motivated Buyers = $

How To Start An Online Business With Less Than $200

How To Market Your Business Online and Offline

Money Blueprint: The Secrets To Creating Instant Wealth

Affiliate Cash: How To Make Money As An Affiliate Marketer

Winning Habits: Getting Rid of A Loser's Mentality

How To Promote Market And Sell Your Kindle Book

AudioBook Profits: How To Make Money by Turning Your Kindle, Paperback and Hardcover Book into Audio.

Money Magnet: How To Use The Laws Of The Universe To Attract Money Into Your Life

Conquering Your Fears

Managing Your Emotions: Critical Steps to Maintaining Control in Life

The Fine Art of Writing The Next Best Seller on Kindle

Fast Cash: 9 Amazing Ways To Make Money Without Having To Work At A Job

Printed in Great Britain
by Amazon